DANGER MOUSE

MOUSE

DECLASSIFIED

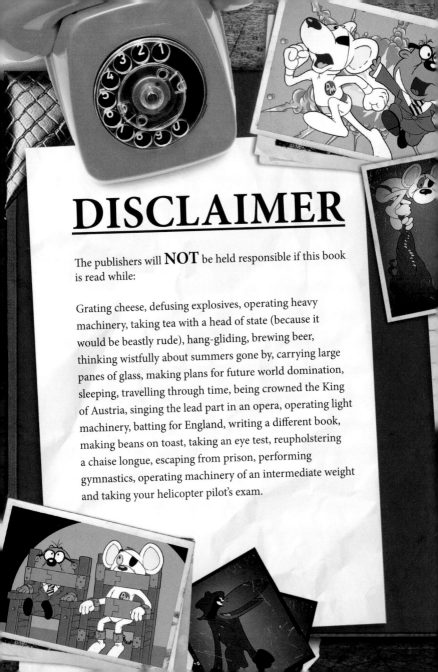

DISCLAIMER

The publishers will **NOT** be held responsible if this book is read while:

Grating cheese, defusing explosives, operating heavy machinery, taking tea with a head of state (because it would be beastly rude), hang-gliding, brewing beer, thinking wistfully about summers gone by, carrying large panes of glass, making plans for future world domination, sleeping, travelling through time, being crowned the King of Austria, singing the lead part in an opera, operating light machinery, batting for England, writing a different book, making beans on toast, taking an eye test, reupholstering a chaise longue, escaping from prison, performing gymnastics, operating machinery of an intermediate weight and taking your helicopter pilot's exam.

DANGER MOUSE

DECLASSIFIED

THE
UNDERCOVER
OPERATIONS
1981 – 1992

IF FOUND PLEASE RETURN TO:
Headquarters:
5 Bedroom Detached
Pillar Box
in Mayfair, London

Virgin BOOKS

TOP SECRET!!!

If you're a baddie, please stop
reading now — close the folder
and hand it back to your nearest
secret service operative.
Thank you!
Penfold x

FILE CONTENTS

QUINN-FLOSSY
— AMO AVOCADOUS —

AUTHOR PREFACE

By Sir Arthur Stuyvesant Quinn-Flossy IV (Bart.)

Dear Reader,

I have been delighted to spend this time with dear Danger Mouse and help to bring his book to fruition. We are both retired gentle-men of a certain age and first met at the Harpo Club in London's Soho. Both a little worse for wear, I fear, ha ha!

Danger Mouse (I have always suspected that he has a different first name, and that Danger is in fact his middle name, but he will not confirm this) sidled up to me with a gin and tonic in hand. Naturally he had heard of my several poetry collections (such as *Banoffee Tango Quagmire* and *Don't Point That Thing at Me You Silly, Silly Sausage*) and in wanting to get a literary work of his own off the ground, I was the chap to approach. I was aghast, however, when he suggested I actually write the thing.

'Naturally dear boy,' I said, 'I won't touch it with a bargepole. Frankly it's beneath me. I'm a poet, don't you see? Why, did I not sign for you a copy of my most recent collection, *Standing in the Bath with an Avocado Sandwich on my Head?*'

'No,' he replied coldly. 'But there's fifty quid in it for you.'

'A hundred,' quoth I. 'Not a penny less.'

'Seventy five,' he said, and with a twinkle in his eye – I shall never forget this – he added the devastating killer blow. 'And an avocado sandwich.'

Well, all of literary London knows my weakness for avocado sandwiches. After that, things took their natural course and now you hold this volume in your hands. Some of the stories are openly preposterous, of course, and in places old DM has rashly embellished what I'm sure were in truth much more mundane adventures.

However trifling a work this is in the grand scheme of things, I am grateful to dear little DM for his modest patronage, which has allowed me to pursue my art – my muse – my true reason for being. My new collection, *Playing Pac-Man in the Romford Wetherspoons with Dismal Jeff*, will appear from Gressingham & Forrester publishers in Spring 2017. I consider it to be a great creative leap forward in my career.

Sir Arthur Stuyvesant Quinn-Flossy IV (Bart.)
May 2016, Romford Wetherspoons

Dear Auntie Flo,

Thank you so much for your lovely Christmas present. I was only just saying to DM the other day that I needed some new hankies, and although the pink flower print is a bit unusual for a boy, I think it goes very well with the floral-pattern waistcoat you bought me last Christmas.

Thanks for asking how things are going here. We've been as busy as ever. We foiled three master-criminals' plots to take over the world last month and I'm determined to get the new living room curtains up before Christmas come what may. We can't just leave the bare curtain pole like that, after all. It's a security issue first and foremost but I don't want the neighbours to catch sight of me doing my morning calisthenics.

Mummy and daddy send their best and say they'd like to see you just as soon as their amateur dramatic effort has come to a close. Apparently, regional newspapers have credited daddy's direction of The Hamsters of Penzance as the finest production to grace the local stage since he directed and starred in Hamster, Prince of Denmark twenty years ago although I thought their production of Hamsters and Dolls was jolly good.

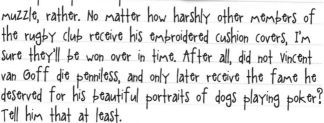

Please tell Uncle Murgatroyd to keep his pecker up. Or his muzzle, rather. No matter how harshly other members of the rugby club receive his embroidered cushion covers, I'm sure they'll be won over in time. After all, did not Vincent van Goff die penniless, and only later receive the fame he deserved for his beautiful portraits of dogs playing poker? Tell him that at least.

I must sign off now because I have to send off the introduction I've written for this new book being published about my adventures, and then I need to get to the hardware store to buy curtain hooks before they close. Thanks again for the rhubarb, bacon and chocolate jam, and in truth I don't need another pot as last year's isn't yet used up!

Your dear nephew,
Penfold

Greetings dear readers!

Although you have followed me and my trusty sidekick **Penfold** on our many adventures over the years, there are several cases so sensitive, so scintillating, so … no, Penfold, not 'silly'! I was going to say, '**secret**'. Anyway, there are many cases that we have never been able to reveal until now, as they have been kept under lock and key at **MI5**. Or is it **MI6**? One of the Mouse Intelligence agencies, anyway.

These were the cases that involved **hugely important issues of national security**, or the wealthiest and most powerful people in the land, so they've had to be kept under wraps for the past **35 years**. Now this restriction has come to an end and the truth can be told at last…

We are delighted at last to reveal these **secret files** to you. Reading them again does bring back memories. London swathed in fog. Sherlock Holmes on the trail of a master criminal. Jack the Ripper stalking the streets… No, wait, that's the 1880s, not the 1980s. My memory grows hazy. But looking through these files reminds me of what exciting times they were.

Can I really have been so **dashing**? Did we really meet all those famous people and foil all these **terrible plots**? Was Penfold really such an utter **chump**? Sorry, Penfold, I forgot you were there for a moment… Come on old friend, let's re-live some of these wonderful memories together.

So, esteemed fans, hold on to your hats and prepare to be **shocked** and **surprised**, **amazed** and **astounded**. Here is the secret dossier of the most **dangerous** and **dastardly plots** we have ever faced.

This is *DANGER MOUSE DECLASSIFIED!*

FAMILY TREE

SIR GERALD MOUSE (b.1557)
Favourite of Queen Elizabeth, Captain of the Chancy Parrot, explorer of the Americas – discoverer of the frisky fruit – poet.

DUKE BAGNOLD CHUTTER QUILPADS FANTASTICO MOUSE (b.1611)
Theatrical impresario – professional ladies' mouse – poet.

HARRISON STERNWELL MOUSE (b.1673)
Shopkeeper – executed in 1694 for killing both his brothers in brawl – poet.

CHESTER FORSTWICK MOUSE (b.1655)
Actor – killed in brawl.

SCRATCHFACE STUMP-MANGLER MOUSE (b.1661)
Barman – killed in brawl.

GERTRUDE HARSCH-BITSCH (NÉE MOUSE) (b.1732)
Housewife – m. Gottfried Harsch-Bitsch.

THOMAS 'ÉGALITÉ, LIBERTÉ, FRATERNITÉ' MOUSE (b.1763)
Famous re-capturer and guillotinier of French Aristocrats.

MATILDA 'RELAXED-VIRTUE' MOUSE (b.1729)
Nun.

SIR JOHN BRILLIANT DAZZLING MOUSE (b. 1760)
Famous rescuer of French Revolutionaries in 1789–90, rumoured to be the Scarlet Pimpermouse.

JEFFREY KAMUTCHNIK MOUSE (b.1823)

US Western pioneer, gunman, railroad builder, inventor of elastic bands and gastric bands, lawmaker, hanging judge and poet.

PEDRO 'EL RATÓN' MOUSE (b.1858)
Mexican revolutionary and poet.

WALTO DISNEO MOUSEO (b.1881)
Father of the Mexican Animation industry (1919–25) – killed by faulty animation of ACME rockets.

Responsible for some of the best mouse films of all time, incl. 'The Mouse King' 'Fantasimouse'

NANOOK OF THE MOUSE (b.1901)
Documentarian and explorer of the Northern Arctic – died from lack of exposure.

CHUCK 'SILLY BOY CHUCKLES' CHANNING-MOUSE (b.1903)
Silent movie comedian. Wrote, starred, directed, did all own stunts.

TERRY MOUSE (b.1934)
Roofer.

He decided to take a step down from his job and landed in next door's garden

THE DAZZLING GOLDEN LIGHT THAT SHINES FROM OUR FINE LEADER MOST WORSHIPPED OF ALL (b.1931)
(official title – Communist ruler of French Guyana 1935–7)
Actual name – Henry Mouse. Pursuits – tennis, backgammon, models, executions.

DANGER MOUSE (b.19__)
SECRET SPECIAL AGENT – born in Willesden.

Oooh, I love stickers!!! ♡

① **LONDON!** 'Hub of Empire, capital of etc etc'

② **MAYFAIR** 'DM's home'

③ **WILLESDEN GREEN** 'Home of the International Ferret Weightlifting Championships 1972-76'

④ **MARIANA TRENCH**
Submarine excitement when we defeated evil explorer Dr Henrik Bunchenpantz, and the only way to get the sub to rise to the surface was for Penfold to eat several tonnes of shrimp that we had gathered! Yum!

⑤ **SEYCHELLES:** 'Absolutely delightful holiday in August '88'

⑥ **ULURU**
We were sent there to capture a vicious giant wallaby that was attacking tourists with venomous boomerangs. The Australian government wanted us to arrest it for being too clichéd! So we threw it a cork hat doused in beer and when it went to sleep we posted it to New Zealand.

⑦ **TRANSYLVANIA**
Would have been an easy mission if it wasn't for the local duck population.

⑧ **MEMORY LANE** ← *very funny, but where do I put the sticker?*
Location of this book

⑨ **ANGEL FALLS**
We visited here because Penfold saw it on the television and he wanted to see where angels fly out from. However when he saw it was the highest waterfall in the world, he wouldn't look over the edge.
I won't look, DM! I won't! You can't make me!

[Also nearby]

⑩ **DEVIL'S FALLS** Populated by bandits, best to avoid

⑪ **MOUNT TAKE-YOUR-TIME** (Uncompleted) Found alongside Mount Rushmore, this is a rock sculpture of America's greatest heroes who did things in good time rather than in a hurry.

14

MAP OF DM's **ADVENTURES** (stickering by me!)

← *Penfold, this is NOT to be blown under any circumstances.*

12 HORN OF AFRICA majestic great big thing like a tuba with ambitions.

13 PIT OF HUMUNGOUS DESPAIR, next to **TOWER OF CERTAIN DEATH**

Very pleasant weekend at this location, no troubles at all, after which we both went to hypnotherapy.

Yes, no unpleasant memories of this at all. No memories at all in fact. Recommended Four stars!

14 HIVE OF THE INFERNAL FIRE-BREATHING MOLLUSCS

Never been there, never wanted to.

Aunty Ruth and Uncle Bert had a weekend there in '75. He had an argument with a rude waiter, she ate a bad pilchard.

15 ALHAMBRA, SPAIN

See, Penfold, the Palace of Granada. They're making more money than Thames Television then!

Penfold, shush!

CASE #1

MISSION CODE NAME:

GET US TO THE CHURCH ON TIME

DATE: July 1981   **REPORTING AGENT:** Danger Mouse

WEATHER: Why on earth do you need to know what the weather is like?

DANGER LEVEL: Quite Dangerous Enough, Thank YOU

URGENCY: URGENT!!

COMMENTS FROM COMMANDING OFFICER:

"SUSPICIOUS ACTIVITY REPORTED IN THE COLD NETHER REGIONS. AND DON'T YOU DARE MAKE ANY REMARKS ABOUT MY PYJAMAS THAT MIGHT MAKE ME SAY SOMETHING I SHALL REGRET. DETECTED ILLICIT COMMUNICATIONS LEAD US TO A REGION IN THE ALPS - NOW GO AND INVESTIGATE!!!

HOW DO I TURN CAPITALS OFF, oh yes"

AUTHORISING SIGNATURE: *Colonel K.*

DANGER MOUSE:

1981, the Royal Wedding. Ah, what a special time. Young, attractive, and dressed all in white…

I looked fantastic as ever. And I saw from the television that soon-to-be Princess Diana looked smashing as well.

But for special agents there was no time for lolling around and watching wedding ceremonies. DM and I had been pursuing a lead in the snowy Alps, where intelligence suggested we were closing in on the stronghold of the artful amphibian himself, BARON GREENBACK!

Yes, thank you, Penfold…

After an unfortunate run-in with a
skier called Eddie the Eagle (even
more short-sighted than Penfold),
we found the Baron's mansion empty.
But we did find an Etch-a-Sketch,
from which Greenback had forgotten
to erase his diabolical plans!

EVIDENCE

Case No. _____ = _____

Date of Collection _July 1981_

Collected By _Dangermouse_

PROPERTY OF
BARON
GREENBACK

Maybe it's me who's shortsighted but to my eyes he doesn't look like an eagle at all →

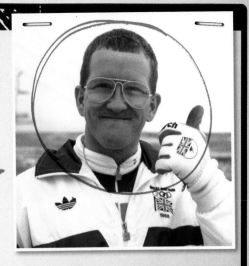

We realised the timer had been set so that it would go off just as the couple were exchanging their vows. What's more, elsewhere in the castle we found receipts for the ingredients for a noxious gas, that would temporarily knock out the Prince and Princess and all their guests.

If their plan unfolded, it would enable Greenback and his dastardly henchman Crow Stiletto to put on their gas masks and steal the Princess's famous diamond tiara.

Racing back to London we crept into St Paul's with all the secrecy that we could just as the royal couple were about to make their pledges.

Which wasn't much!

But what was that horrible gassy smell? Were we too late? Or had Penfold's nerves got the better of him?…

He who smelt it, dealt it, Chief! ☺

Luckily we were able to thwack the Baron and Stiletto back into the box they had themselves sent, and then place that box on Eddie the Eagle's skis, and send it flying out of the cathedral at the last moment, to explode in the fresh air!

COLONEL K

:::::::::INCOMING MESSAGE:::::::::

Jolly good work, DM! The whole world was watching and it wouldn't have done for anything to go wrong in this wedding, or even marriage! Long may it last, may I say!

SECRET SERVICE

INSURANCE RENEWAL FORM

NAME OF DRIVER:

D. Mouse, esq.

OTHER DRIVERS INSURED UNDER THIS POLICY:

P. Fold (hamster)

DATE OF BIRTH:

None of your business

VEHICLE INSURED:

Mark III – Secret Service vehicle

NUMBER OF INSURANCE CLAIMS OVER LAST YEAR:

194

WAS YOUR LAST CLAIM DUE TO (PLEASE TICK):

- ☐ Other driver's liability.
- ☐ Technical failure.
- ☐ Entire world's electrical appliances becoming possessed by need to float into space and form a giant robot.
- ☐ Penfold, yet again.
- ☐ Attack from sentient meteorite with a lousy taste in puns.
- ☐ Tsunami of poison custard.
- ☐ Super-villain wielding weapon that threatens to turn planet inside out.
- ☑ Irascible mega-lizard.

If you answered "irascible mega-lizard" to the previous question, was its bad temper owing to actions you had yourself personally undertaken?

- ☐ Yes
- ☐ No
- ☑ Other (Please specify): *Both yes and no. We shot lasers into its eyes, but when he turned up he was in a decidedly bad mood to start with. Six of one and half a dozen of the other, I'd say.*

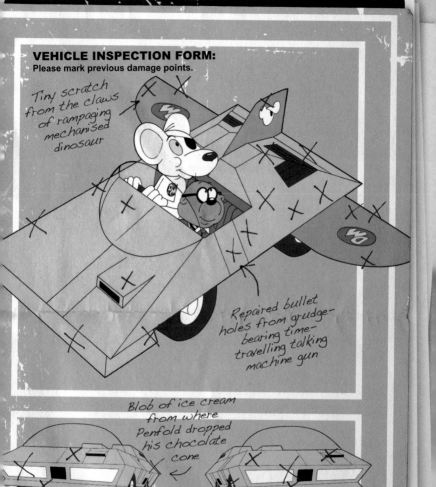

VEHICLE INSPECTION FORM:
Please mark previous damage points.

Tiny scratch from the claws of rampaging mechanised dinosaur

Repaired bullet holes from grudge-bearing time-travelling talking machine gun

Blob of ice cream from where Penfold dropped his chocolate cone

DRIVER'S SIGNATURE:

Danger Mouse

POLICY:

REJECTED!

CASE #2

MISSION CODE NAME:

ASHES TO ASHES

DATE: Summer 1982

REPORTING AGENT: Danger Mouse

LOCATION: LONDON! Metropolis of magnificent magnetism! Huge hotspot of hopscotchery! (At least I assume it is. It must be, if you think about it.)

FINISH: Marble-effect

DANGER LEVEL: So DANGEROUS I've changed my first name and last name to DANGEROUS, meaning my name is now DANGEROUS DANGEROUS McSporran DANGEROUS (McSporran is my mother's maiden name)

COMMENTS FROM COMMANDING OFFICER:

"SPLENDID WELL-EARNED DAY OFF FOR US SECRET AGENTS - WATCHING THE CRICKET AT LORDS! NICE GLASS OF PORT WITH LUNCH, CLAPPING THE BATSMEN IN AND OUT, THAT HERO IAN BOTHAM TAKING THE AUSSIES TO TASK, SUN IN THE SKY! COULD ONE ASK FOR ANYTHING MORE? EXCEPT PERHAPS FOR PENFOLD TO STOP RUNNING TO THE TOILET ALL THE TIME BECAUSE HE'S DRUNK TOO MUCH SQUASH? HOWEVER, IN THE MIDDLE OF THE AFTERNOON SESSION IT SEEMS SOMETHING VERY RUM IS AFOOT AND WE NEED OUR TOP SECRET AGENT (NOT YOU PENFOLD, SORRY) TO INVESTIGATE!"

AUTHORISING SIGNATURE: *Colonel K.*

DANGER MOUSE:

The Australian players had suddenly
fielded this enormous fast bowler, who
looked like Mr Universe, and had an accent
that didn't sound Australian at all. After
bowling each ball he intoned gravely,
'I'll be back…' My suspicions were aroused
when his first three balls were so fast
they ripped through the batsmen's bats
leaving holes surrounded by flames and
smoke. One of them carried on through the
wall of the stadium to knock someone out
in the carpark over the road. 'Flamin'
'eck!' said Penfold, and I agreed.

This strong-arm chap certainly seemed a match for
our boys. Instead of using a traditional overarm delivery,
he kept removing his hand, inserting the ball into his
wrist and firing it back out like a cannon. Also, when
a ball being thrown back from a fielder struck him in
the face, it knicked his cheekbone and revealed he was
partly made of metal. 'Ere,' I said. 'That's not entirely
cricket, is it?' 'Not even a little bit, Penfold,' said DM.

So we snuck into the Australian
dressing room disguised as cricket
balls where we saw an appalling sight.
Instead of bags of clothes and cricket
pads, there were only giant sparking
plugs where they had been recharged.
They were all robots! Pinned to the
wall where the teamsheet should be
was their secret plan: to eliminate
the English team and replace the famous
Ashes with radioactive space dust!
'That's DEFINITELY not cricket!'
said Penfold. 'Yes, thank you Penfold,
I think we've made that joke now,'
I replied.

We reported back to Colonel K, who was snoozing
with port stains around his lips, and he said to get
our trusty scientist Dr Squawkencluck involved —
and as quick as possible, or else our boys would
be slaughtered. 'And we wouldn't want blood
on our hands, Colonel!' I said. 'Not that, old boy,
I mean in the score!'

Dr Squawkencluck arrived with a spotty
young herbert in tow, who he said was a
computer whizz called Bill Gates. This
Gates fellow told us to switch out the
ball for one of his own creation, which
contained a computer virus. 'Don't like
the sound of a virus, DM,' said Colonel
K, 'I haven't had my jabs, you know.'

But brave old DM got an umpire's
uniform on and went out on the pitch
to change the ball all right. When it
activated, all the virus-infected robots
flew into the upper atmosphere
and used their poisonous space dust
on the spaceship from which Baron
Greenback was controlling them, making
it explode with a mighty boom which
was, however, inaudible to us. The real
Australian players were discovered tied
up in the back of a van and the
game continued as though nothing had
happened! Now that really IS cricket!

PENFOLD'S LIST OF
THINGS THAT ARE
NOT CRICKET

Being a rotten egg.
Badminton.
The history of saws.
The Bohemian Tree-
dwelling Vampire Bat.
Running out of clean
underpants.
Baron Greenback.

————

PENFOLD'S LIST OF THINGS
THAT ARE CRICKET

Cricket.

Cricketing Terminator Robot

BOWLING AVERAGES

Bowling speed: 0-150 mph in 0.03 seconds

Wickets: 3 caught, 7 stumped, 348 retired hurt / incinerated

BATTING AVERAGES

Average score: infinity (not-out so far in entire career)

Balls destroyed: 766

Bats destroyed: 465

Bowlers destroyed: 27 (26 by accident, 1 after argument over superiority of Australian robot cricketers over robot cricketers from other nations)

Weather satellites destroyed by sixes over bowler's arm: 1

OTHER STATS

Violent rampages: 1 (faulty wiring)

Favourite food: oil

Least favourite food: oil

Brushes teeth with: oil

Dreams about: oil

Most Beloved Cartoon Character: Olive Oyl

You know, Penfold, in the original series we did scenes in the dark like this to save money on animation cells.
But you see the way printing works, it actually costs more to have most of the page made black like this.
Funny, isn't it, what lengths people will go to for a little bit of nostalgia?

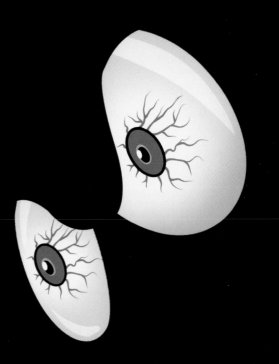

CASE #3

MISSION CODE NAME:

THE ATTIRE STRIKES BACK!

DATE: November 1982

REPORTING AGENT: Danger Mouse

LOCATION: LONDON! Focus of fashion and pillar of pulchritude!

HEIGHT: 0'3'' in smart shoes

DANGER LEVEL: More dangerous that I would care to say

URGENCY: SUPRA-URGENT

COMMENTS FROM COMMANDING OFFICER:

"TERRIFYING TIMES - THE NATION'S SHOULDER PADS HAVE RISEN UP AGAINST US! THERE ARE MILLIONS OF THEM IN THE SKY, BLOCKING OUT THE SUN! THREATENING THE VERY FABRIC OF OUR EXISTENCE (NOT TO MENTION OF OUR SUITS)! AND DISTURBING THE CRICKET! GET OUT THERE AND FIND OUT WHAT THE CRIVENS IS GOING ON! I'VE GOT TICKETS FOR THE THIRD TEST!"

AUTHORISING SIGNATURE: *Colonel K.*

DANGER MOUSE:

It all began with an invitation to a
special exciting event - the launch of a
new, fourth television channel! Colonel
K muttered that it was nonsense and the
idea of more than three channels would
never catch on. But nevertheless we
were there, to watch the filming of an
exciting new programme about spelling,
called Countdown.

When the host's chair turned round, who did we see in
it but that fiend's-best-friend Stiletto! The two teams
were all trussed up and gagged, and when the first set
of letters appeared, they spelled

D E S T R U C T I

Penfold spent the thirty seconds exclaiming
what a fun game this was and trying to work
out what the answer could be. But Stiletto
noticed he'd missed two letters off the
end, and added them in pen.

Then Penfold cried 'Oh cripes!' and
Stiletto said what we had all been
thinking: 'That's right, my friends!
This spells …'

D E S T R U C T I ON

An alarm sounded and we went outside, only to see
hundreds of city folk hanging in the air, held aloft
by their own shoulder pads! Then the shoulder pads
all broke free of the clothes they were in and shot
into the sky, leaving the people to bounce down
painfully on their backsides!

We soon heard that this gargantuan
grotesquerie of gallivanting garments
had gathered 100 km above the earth, in
the Greenbackosphere. There was only one
conclusion - they must be under the control
of the flying laboratory belonging to the
arch-villainous Baron Greenback!

Oh not him AGAIN. Can't we have another villain?
A less dangerous one perhaps?

No sooner did we learn this than we
visited US President Ray-Gun in the Oval
Office. Colonel K was most disappointed,
as he thought we had set out to the
Oval, and wanted to hear the score in
the test against Sri Lanka. We had heard
mention of the billions of dollars that
President Ray-Gun had invested in his
magisterial Star Wars project and now
was the time to put it into action!

Imagine how upset we were to get there and find all
he had was a couple of X-wings, a Millennium Falcon and
an AT-AT Walker, fresh out of their boxes! The only
explanation he would offer was, 'Why, boys, you don't
know how expensive these are second hand? That's a
brand new Corellian Corvette!' Then he disappeared under
the desk with a craft in each hand, yelling, 'Pew pew
pew! I got you! Oh no, we're hit, we're going down!
EeeeeeeeeeaaaarrrrrowwwmmKABLAM!' Looking at him
playing with his toys, DM said that at least America could
never again be cursed with such an unintelligent President.

So we were thrown back on our wits. Next thing we knew, Greenback had made an announcement, taking responsibility for the outbreak once and for all, and giving his terms: that he at once be made Emperor of the entire planet, or he would unleash shoulder pad destruction (or rather, 'destructi') upon the capitals of the world, one by one, via his Space Invaders!

However while waiting for our response, on the computer screen within his craft Baron Silas Greenback suddenly saw dozens of huge craft approaching, containing countless heavily armed soldiers ready to board and arrest him. In a panic, he grabbed a parachute and bailed out.

But there was no one there at all! You see, we realised we couldn't overwhelm the Baron's forces on our own. So while we were in America DM said why not pop over to those terribly clever chaps at Lucasfilm's Industrial Light and Magic, who did such a jolly good job on The Empire Strikes Back, and see if they can rustle up some special effects? Which they did, and it saved the day!

YOUR GUIDE TO
POWER DRESSING
for the Modern Boardroom

Power hungry hair
(use as much hairspray
as possible)

Shoulder pads
(bulletproof)

Caustic collar

Ruthless lapels

Business-like
cuffs

Ambitious elbows

Heartless hem

'Greed is good' heels

Just a thought, DM. If Channel 4
is this good, imagine how good
a Channel 5 would be...

Colonel K's
New Year's Eve
Fancy Dress Party

Let's Ring In
1983!

We were
supposed to
dress as an
event from
history. I
decided to come
as a medieval
cowboy!

I just threw
on a few
things I had
lying around in
my wardrobe...

I remember I had to put an awful lot of effort into my costume — you can't buy a potato sack without buying the potatoes too.

I had mash with every meal for three months. Baked potato and mash was the worst one...

Penfold went as the Irish potato famine.

CASE #4

MISSION CODE NAME:

A HOLE IN THE OH-NO-ZONE!

DATE: July 1985   **REPORTING AGENT:** Danger Mouse

LOCATION: The Earth's Atmosphere

HIGHEST CHARTING POSITION: 13 (Portuguese singles chart)

DANGER LEVEL: Gives new definition to the word DANGEROUS

URGENCY: TREMENDOUSLY URGENT

COMMENTS FROM COMMANDING OFFICER:

"FRIGHTENING HAPPENINGS AND JITTERY STOMACHS THE WORLD OVER, DM! SCARCELY A MOMENT AFTER WE'VE GOT IT IN OUR HEADS THAT WE JOLLY WELL NEED THIS OZONE STUFF, SOMEONE'S GONE AND SAWN A HOLE OUT OF IT THE SIZE OF A FOOTBALL FIELD. RUGBY FOOTBALL THAT IS, NOT THAT NEWFANGLED NONSENSE WITH A ROUND BALL. GET OUT THERE AND BRING OUR OZONE BACK, SO WE DON'T ALL TURN INTO OMELETTES!"

AUTHORISING SIGNATURE: .... *Colonel K.* ....

DANGER MOUSE:

It seemed that Baron Greenback was
up to his old tricks again. Not
only did it sound like the sort
of scheme he'd get into, but when
we investigated, we discovered the
only Giant Atmospheric Saw that
had been rented out recently by
the World Altering Tools Company
had been signed for by him.
Dastardly doings indeed!

We looked up where the hole had been cut — directly
above north-west London — and pondered why he would
choose such a spot. 'Of course DM, I've got it!' I said.
'He's trying to drive down prices in the area so
he can spend his ill-gotten gains on a maisonette!'

I told Penfold not to be so silly. 'Haven't you noticed what's happening in the area ju[st] tomorrow?' I asked. 'There are seventy thousand people coming to Wembley Stadium for Live Aid! They'll be cooked alive!' 'Oh crumbs!' said Penfold.

It seemed the tyrannical toad wanted to use the distraction to steal all the funds collected for Live Aid. But DM said that in order to succeed, he had to be there himself to issue the threat on live television. So we disguised ourselves as Elton John's wigs and snuck in...

As we were hiding in Madonna's wardrobe, we came across two utterly strange white protuberances, which gave me an idea…

PENFOLD IS ACTUALLY PLAYING 'THE SUN HAS GOT HIS HAT ON'.

LIVE AID

WEMBLEY STADIUM LONDON

1985 – TRANSCRIPT OF INTERVIEW WITH BOB GELDOF:

BBC Reporter:
So, Mr Geldof, what do you hope to achieve with this concert?

B. Geldof: Well I [BLEEP] [BLEEP] [BLEEPING] [BLEEP] because it's [BLEEPING] [BLEEP] [BLEEP] [BLEEP] if you [BLEEP] [BLEEP] the [BLEEPING] [BLEEP], and I think everyone can see that's the case.

BBC Reporter: Er, well, okay — yes, of course. And what difference do you hope this makes long term?

B. Geldof: Of course I [BLEEPING] [BLEEP] [BLEEP] if anyone [BLEEP] [BLEEP] [BLEEBLEEBLEEP!] [BLEEP] but there's a lot to [BLEEP] [BLEEP] [BLEEP] if we can [BLEEPING] [BLEEP] and I [BLEEPING] believe that is [BLEEPING] possible.

BBC Reporter: Mr Geldof, we have to leave it there. Thank you for your time.

B. Geldof: [BLEEP]

When the gargoyle Greenback went
on stage to state his demands,
we threw these enormous conical
contrivances over his head,
baffling him and making him trip
and fall off the stage!

Once we'd disabled Greenback with Madonna's
brassiere, DM found the missing ozone in the
boot of his car. In a trice we transferred it to
the Mark III, zoomed it back up into the sky
and sewed it back in place. We'd saved the day,
the crowds cheered and the concert carried on
without us! In case you're under any illusions though,
we did not solve hunger, which does
most definitely continue to be an issue.

COLONEL K

::::::::::INCOMING MESSAGE::::::::::
Good show DM! We really showed the
abominable amphibian what we're made of,
what? I say "we" – you did a lot of the heavy
lifting. But there was a pretty hairy moment
where I nearly got locked in the executive
toilet and missed the afternoon tea trolley.
Good teamwork I say!

JOIN THE DANGER MOUSE FAN CLUB!

Ever wanted to join your favourite SUPER SPY on his wild and wonderful adventures?

Well you CAN'T, they're much too dangerous and the insurance would be a jolly nuisance. Why would you even suggest such a thing? HOWEVER you can keep UP TO DATE and get the INSIDE GOSSIP on all things to do with Danger Mouse by joining his exclusive FAN CLUB!

Simply send a self-addressed envelope to the below address with a postal order for £1.20 and you might receive:*

- A BADGE declaring that you are an exclusive member of the DANGER MOUSE DANGER SQUAD!

- A LICENCE signed by the WHITE WONDER himself, giving permission to perform and commit acts of derring do and amazing heroism at any time!**

- A MONTHLY NEWSLETTER containing exclusive interviews, pictures, titbits, puzzles and more!

- A sense of SELF SATISFACTION at being able to tell your friends they are jolly well inferior because they're not members of the exclusive club!

- A personal letter SIGNED*** by Danger Mouse himself welcoming you to the fold!

- ANNUAL MEET UP of the club, usually at the scout hall, Nether Pondlake, Rutland! (Knock if no answer to bell, it's temperamental.) Free squash and biscuit provided (ONE EACH.)

Send SAE to:
Johnny Pargeter, the Old Vicarage, Nether Pondlake, Rutland.

*You might not.   **The Danger Mouse Fan Club Corporation is indemnified against any legal action created by acts of derring do. Please act with caution and consult your pharmacist.   ***Not signed.

CASE #5

MISSION CODE NAME:

A NIGHTMARE ON REGENT STREET

DATE: December 1985

REPORTING AGENT: Danger Mouse

LOCATION: LONDON! International Centre of Excellence and Location of the Stoke Newington Female Bat Impersonation Society!

FLAVOUR: Raspberry Ripple and Marmite

DANGER LEVEL: As dangerous as you can imagine x2

URGENCY: ULTRA URGENT

COMMENTS FROM COMMANDING OFFICER:

"CHRISTMAS SHOPPING IS IN FULL FLOW AND FATHER CHRISTMAS IS ON THE HORIZON. BUT WHAT'S THIS? ALL THE VIDEO CASSETTES IN THE WORLD HAVE BEEN REPLACED BY A GHASTLY INFLUX OF VIDEO NASTIES - AWFUL FILMS WHERE PEOPLE DO BEASTLY THINGS WITH AXES, CHAINSAWS, TENNIS RACQUETS AND I DON'T KNOW WHAT. THE PEOPLE ARE IN UPROAR, AND THE ROAR SAYS: SEND IN DANGER MOUSE! TOO RIGHT, AND TO WHICH I ADD, PENFOLD, YOU'D BETTER GO WITH 'IM"

AUTHORISING SIGNATURE: *Colonel K.*

AGENT'S MISSION NOTES

DANGER MOUSE:

When we hunted down the boxes
that all the replacement video
cassettes had been unpacked
from, they bore a sinister
return address: that of a tall,
gaunt castle in the middle of a
mysterious forest. When I said we
had to go, Penfold suddenly seemed
to develop a sharp cough. And a
sprained earlobe. And a cracked
pancreas. But I won't accept any
feeble excuses when the country
calls. So we were off!

There we were, tiptoeing through the silent dark
forest, when a terrible shadow loomed above us,
accompanied by a mighty roar. I covered my eyes
and DM let out a shriek. 'Good LORD, Penfold! What a
smell, you must learn to control yourself!' I apologised
wholeheartedly, and wholetrouseredly, and we went to
investigate what was ahead of us.

We discovered a bunch of delightful inhabitants gathered around a camp fire, who described themselves as 'Care Bears'. They were friendly and happy, with lovely brightly coloured fur, and it was just the light from the camp fire throwing shadows on the rocks. When we asked what had made the terrible roar, we were introduced to Cuddly Bear, who was watching *Life on Earth* on a telly by the fireside. 'I LOVE David Attenborough!' he said, with hearts springing from his eyes.

We asked for directions to the big scary castle. Unfortunately, they gave us them. When we got there we pushed open the doors of the castle as quietly as we could. But that didn't stop a whole lot of frightening things popping out — a ghost! A falling axe! A trapdoor springing open!!!!

When Penfold had stopped screaming I pointed out that the ghost was no more than a sheet on a stick, and that the axe was made of plastic. In fact, reaching behind a curtain I grabbed hold of none other than television prankster Jeremy Beagle, up to his old tricks again!

When we got it out of him Mr Beagle admitted that the video nasty hoax was supposed to scare the audiences of Britain so much they needed a light entertainer like him on the airwaves again. He broke away from our grasp but was so disorientated he ran into the wall, making a portrait fall on him. His head burst through the canvas and he sat there looking dazed. 'You know what?' I quipped. 'You've been framed!'

Hush, Penfold.

Now Penfold, be careful not to step over that ledge...
Bit too late for that, chief!

YOU ARE DANGER. YOU ARE EXCITEMENT.
YOU FEAR NOTHING.

YOU THRIVE ON ADRENALIN,
AND LIVE FOR RISK. YOU ARE A JUNGLE CAT,
READY TO POUNCE.

ESSENCE
OF
DANGER

ESSENCE OF DANGER:
THE NEW SCENT FROM THE MOST FAMOUS AND BRILLIANT
SUPER-SPY THE WORLD HAS EVER KNOWN.

Combining exotic ingredients to undeniably pungent effect, 'WHIFF' by Pongfold is an exciting new scent that's sure to get a strong reaction. Whether used as a cologne before setting out on a romantic evening out, or poured behind the fridge to get rid of an infestation of cockroaches, there's one thing that's for sure: Penflod's 'WHIFF' has a strong effect that you will find difficult to forget!

CASE #6

MISSION CODE NAME:

SPACE CRUSADERS

DATE: March 1986	**REPORTING AGENT:** Danger Mouse

LOCATION: LONDON! Capital of commerce, cultural crux and core of commonwealth!

COSTUME: Mexican peasant

REASON FOR COSTUME: Margaritas at lunchtime

DANGER LEVEL: What sort of a question is that?

URGENCY: SUPER URGENT

COMMENTS FROM COMMANDING OFFICER:

"DIABOLICALLY TERRIFYING APPARITION ABOVE HYDE PARK - SERRIED RANKS OF ALIEN SPACE SHIPS. BLASTING (EXCUSE MY LANGUAGE, DM, BUT IT'S A BALLY EMERGENCY), BLASTING I SAY, AWAY AT THE BELOVED LANDMARKS OF THE CAPITAL! BEASTLY THINGS ARE INVADING FROM SPACE! TO GIVE THEM A PITHY NAME I SHALL CALL THEM 'INVADING SPACE CRAFT … FROM SPACE'. YES, THAT'S A GOOD NAME. IS IT THAT TIME ALREADY? MY TABLE WILL BE READY FOR LUNCH. HOW DO I TURN OFF THIS VOICE RECORDER, AH Y-"

AUTHORISING SIGNATURE: *Colonel K.*

The moment I caught sight of this terrible threat, I knew exactly what to do. Move to Mexico and change my name to Manuel de Incognito. However before I had a chance to call my travel agent,

DANGER MOUSE: DM stole my passport.

It seemed obvious that the threat could not be countered from the ground. The only way was to get up in space as well. I had heard that soon to launch was a Russian rocket called the Spudnik. In order to get to know the Russians, we enlisted MI-6's most dangerous retired agent: James Bones, a.k.a. 0070.

EXTRACT FROM INTERVIEW:

DM: This chap makes Colonel K look like a whippersnapper!

Agent 0070: (rousing himself from slumber): Snapper? Well okay, but I'd rather have salmon, or dover sole. With a nice bottle of …
(snore)

After we'd questioned him closely
for several hours, we plugged in
his hearing aid, which really made
him pay attention. Then within
minutes he told us how to access
the Mir Space Station …

EXTRACT FROM INTERVIEW:

DM: Tell us about the Mir Space
Station

Agent 0070: It's not a mere space
station. It's rather wonderful
in fact … could someone undo my
corset … (snore)

We all got propelled up into space on the
Russian Spudnik, some of us more reluctantly
than others, where DM really began to get
his teeth into his investigation.

I have made this to demonstrate the drama of the mission! Hope it helps...

As we travelled through the infinite darkness of space, and pondered the endless, impervious nothingness that was in front of us, and the beauty of the cosmos … I thought, HANG ON. That's Baron Greenback!

And so clever old DM spotted our old nemesis at the centre of the alien invasion. In a trice we had invaded his ship, with old Agent 0070 doddering along behind on his jet mobility scooter.

'You fools!' Greenback cried, when we broke into his lair. 'I shall destroy you with my alien army!' But at that moment the timer ran out on his 'Evil Invading Alien Army-Controlling Machine'. He patted his pockets and cursed himself for buying a Refresher Bar before coming on board.
'You'll spoil your dinner!' I said. We dashed forward to grab him but he dived into an escape pod and fired himself into space.

'Dash it all, DM!' I said. 'The villain has escaped us again!' But he didn't seem at all worried. 'I wouldn't want to be in his shoes, you know,' he said.
'Look what he's steered himself towards' —
'Oh crumbs!' I said. 'Asteroids!

Rather than trying to take over the world, he should relax. Perhaps play one of those modern computer games.

EVIL INVADING ALIEN ARMY-CONTROLLING MACHINE

COINS ACCEPTED:
£1, 50P, 20P, 10P

ALIEN CURRENCY
NOT ACCEPTED.

DO NOT INSERT ITEMS
THAT ARE NOT COINS
INTO THIS DEVICE.

ANY MALFUNCTION,
PLEASE CALL 01-78-7981
AND ASK FOR JUDY
(DOESN'T WORK TUESDAYS).

COLONEL K

:::::::::::INCOMING MESSAGE:::::::::::

AH, YES, VIDEO GAMES, WHAT? I KNOW SOME
PEOPLE LOVE 'EM! BUT HAVING TO DEAL WITH
LEGIONS OF EVIL ALIEN CRAFT INVADING THE
EARTH HELLBENT ON DESTRUCTION?
I GET ENOUGH OF THAT AT WORK!

Remember when we both decided to get pets, Penfold? That was one time when you certainly thought it out better than I did...

How are you getting on with your pet, Penfold? Surely it must be time to feed him?

Oh, Tinny the tin? No, he's quite alright. Getting on better than ever. Hardly seems to need feeding at all. He looks so restful where he is — I hardly like to disturb him — la-de-da.

CASE #7

MISSION CODE NAME:

BACK TO THE PHEW-CHER

DATE: March 1986	**REPORTING AGENT:** Danger Mouse

LOCATION: The Wild, Wild, Wild, Wild West.

COLOUR: Taupe

DANGER LEVEL: Take my word for it that it is DANGEROUS

URGENCY: TERRIFICALLY URGENT

COMMENTS FROM COMMANDING OFFICER:

"TERRIBLE NEWS FROM ACROSS THE ATLANTIC! PRESIDENT RAY-GUN HAS UP AND VANISHED! THE STABILITY OF THE WORLD IS AT STAKE! JOLLY GET OUT THERE AND FIND THE CHAP TOOT SWEET! OH LOOK, A PIGEON. MARGERY! COME IN HERE AND LOOK AT THIS! A PIGEON ON MY WINDOWSILL! AH, I'M STILL RECORDING, HOW EMBARR—"

AUTHORISING SIGNATURE: *Colonel K.*

DANGER MOUSE:

Arriving at the scene of the crime, Penfold and I followed flaming car tracks through the desert until we came across a rather angry robot holding a tennis racquet. From his breastplate we saw he was called John Mech-enroe. No sooner did we ask directions than he started arguing with us, yelling that he did not BELIEVE it, he just could not BELIEVE it, and so on. Dreadful bore.

Sooner or later however he directed us towards the abode of a wild-haired scientist called Dr Emmett Brown. He told us that President Ray-Gun had been kidnapped by Robot Cowboys Clint Eastwood and Yul Brynner, who'd taken him into the future to create a Wild West theme park.

At this point Penfold said, 'Ah well, can't be helped. Time to go home, then …' But I soon put a stop to that. Working together overnight, Doctor Emmett Brown and I retrofitted the Mark III to travel through time. Despite Penfold trying to hide in a dustbin and pretending to be the contents of a packet of bacon, we were soon shooting through the time-stream on our way to rescue the president!

It took DM a little while to get the hang of the controls. First he took us to seventeenth century America, where I nearly got burned as a witch. Next we found ourselves in Queen Victoria's boudoir, and she was certainly not amused, by 'eck! Then we popped by the 1924 Olympics and watched the races made famous by Chariots of Fire. Crumbs, it was exciting!

Finally I got used to the controls and we zipped into the future, located the robots and trapped them by dropping a giant extra-strength magnet between them, locking them together forever. President Ray-Gun was most relieved to be rescued - but his gratitude stopped short of allowing Penfold any of his Star Wars collection.

Hang on a minute Chief, if people are reading this in the future, in 2016, say, it will be 'back to the future of the past' for them. Or 'back to the future that would become the past'. Oh dear, this is making my brain zz. Can someone please ask that nice Professor Hawking to explain?

INVASION BY POISONOUS GRASSHOPPERS STOPPED BY WATER CANNON FILLED WITH CHOCOLATE MILKSHAKE

Cannon Operated by Anonymous Hero

Dramatic scenes in Washington yesterday as giant, venomous insects appeared and appeared to threaten human civilisation. The alien crafts appeared shortly before tea time and made an enormous racket, issuing their demands before being blasted into smithereens by a mystery assailant wielding a world-saving water cannon loaded with delicious chocolate thickshake.

Mouse Seen Fleeing Area to Safety

BARON GREENBACK'S ARMY OF VENGEFUL MICROWAVE OVENS HALTED BY BROADCAST FROM RADIO TOWER

EXCLUSIVE

Tiny rodent wearing eye-patch spotted in area

As you can see I'm much too humble to claim credit for my heroic actions. Certainly wouldn't want them written about in a book or a television series or anything. →

the 20?1-02 season.

?ayed ??? ??? side ii.

World War Averted After Giant Inflated Octopus Armed With Galactic Spud Gun Disappears Over Surrey Downs

Nearby Sightings of Nail Gun-Wielding Mouse Unconfirmed

ed

l are

't

eir

she

that

es to

A

me

aga

H.

Ly

in

ling

CASE #8

MISSION CODE NAME:

LOST IN TV

DATE: August 1986

REPORTING AGENT: Danger Mouse

LOCATION: LONDON! Melting pot of mightiness, centre of sensationalism!

COLOUR: Heliotrope

DANGER LEVEL: DANGEROUS, very DANGEROUS indeed

URGENCY: SUPERLATIVELY URGENT

COMMENTS FROM COMMANDING OFFICER:

"TERRIBLE EVENTS, DM! NO SOONER DO I SIT DOWN TO MY TV DINNER LAST NIGHT AND SWITCH ON THE BOX THAN THAT ROTTER GREENBACK APPEARS! ON *MURDER SHE WROTE*, IF YOU PLEASE! IN THE PLACE OF ANGELA LANSBURY! HE EVEN WORE HER GLASSES AND WIG! AND NOW HE'S ON *DALLAS* AND *SESAME STREET* TOO! HE'S TAKEN OVER TELEVISION. YOU HAVE TO FIND HIM AND STOP HIM! THE TOAD'S A MENACE!"

AUTHORISING SIGNATURE: *Colonel K.*

DANGER MOUSE:

First thing we did was to meet up
with a chap who knew TV inside-out,
a certain Mr Hassle-Hoff who drove a
talking car (which certainly alarmed
Penfold). We also had some friends of
his on our side - an enormous green
chap who said we wouldn't like him
when he's angry, a band of vigilante
mercenaries (who had escaped from
a military stockade after being
imprisoned for a crime they didn't
commit) and a very resourceful chap in
a mullet who claimed to be able to make
weapons out of any household items.

With this exciting band by our side, we broke into
Central TV studios while they were recording an
episode of Blockbusters. The only contestant was
Greenback, of course, and the questions he was
facing asked by Stiletto were things like, 'What
is the capital of England?' and 'What is ten plus
twelve?' Pretty difcult stuff!

Don't be silly, Penfold, the
questions were deliberately easy. And
when the curtain drew back and we saw
the prize on offer - it was all the
money in the world, placed in a large
gold cup! With that in his control
Greenback would be unstoppable!

Just at that moment I was eating a Twister, and
it slipped out of my hand and fell down the neck
of the nice Dr David Banner who had been standing
in front of me. He jumped up and down and
claimed that this was his best shirt, and he'd just
had it cleaned. The next thing I knew he had gone,
and been replaced by the green, enormous chap we
had met earlier, who started furiously rampaging
all over the place!

The Incredible Hulk rampaged onto the
set of Blockbusters and when Stiletto
tried to tell him to clear off,
he hoofed him through a window and
clear into the next county, in fact!
Then he rampaged off to the next
studio, muttering something almost

unintelligible about 'that idiot Teenwolf'. This left the way clear for me to step in as host, and ask Greenback some proper questions.

EXTRACT OF TRANSCRIPT FROM BLOCKBUSTERS

Episode #375, March 1986:

HOST: What is the national dish of Yugoslavia?

GREENBACK: What? I don't know that!

HOST: Oh dear. The answer was of course 'pljeskavica', a ground-meat patty. Question two: what is the furthest northerly point in the Soviet Union?

GREENBACK: But that's impossible! How could I know th—

HOST: What a shame. The answer is Cape Fligely, just 911 km from the North Pole, named after the Austrian cartographer August von Fligely. Question three, and you need this to stay in: who was the second reserve goalkeeper for West Germany in this summer's Mexico World Cup?

GREENBACK: Oh! Wait! Was it Uli Stein?

HOST: Oh, so close. No, I'm afraid it was Borussia Dortmund's Eike Immel!

GREENBACK: Eike Immel! Of course it was! Curse you, White Wonder, for your interfering ways! You shall live to regret this!

HOST: Oh dear – threatening the host means that it's into the gunk tank for you!

GREENBACK: But this show doesn't have a gunk tank!

MACGYVER (appearing over Greenback's shoulder): In fact, I just fashioned one from dental floss, paper clips, a mattress and a vat of paint left over from episodes of Hartbeat.

GREENBACK: Noooooooooooo! (Splurge)

THE GREENBACK TELEVISION SHOW QUIZ

While he was on the rampage through the world of television, that Verdigris Villain and Emerald Evildoer Baron Greenback dressed up as a host of different TV characters. Can you correctly identify the devilish disguises of that Lime-hued Liability?

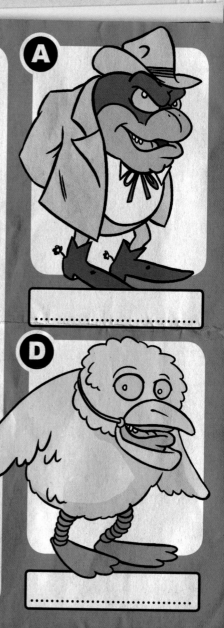

A

....

D

....

....

....

....

I seem to remember finding school a doddle! I showed them what was what all right! Ah isn't it fun to look back on those days, Penfold?

Pupil:

D. Mouse

ACADEMIC

since 1880

Marks:

Literature	A+
Maths	A+
History	A+
Science	A+
Geography	A+
PE:	A++

Teacher's comments:

Master Mouse is the finest student one could possibly meet. He's head of all the sports teams, has taken the lead role in the school play, and has created a new menu for the school canteen which has led to it being awarded a Michelin star. In fact, he's only been here one term, but I have resigned, and made him headmaster!

Signed:

HEAD BOY

Oh! It was ghastly, DM. It was like being trapped running in a wheel that never stops! ☹

Well, you are a hamster, Perhaps you should get used to that ...

Pupil:

Penfold

Marks:

Literature	D-
Maths	D-
History	C
Science	C
Geography	D
PE:	D-

Teacher's comments:

I know young Master Penfold is a student at this school because I can see his name here on the register. Dashed if I can remember him though. Ah yes! Isn't he the tall gangling Irish lad, who slurps his soup? Hmm. No, that chap's called Hanrahan. Perhaps he's the limping Russian boy with a lisp. Nnnno, that's Kropotsky. Ah yes! Penfold! Now I've got him. Not much to say I'm afraid but at least I have filled out this form now.

Signed:

CASE #9

MISSION CODE NAME:

RUSSIAN AROUND

DATE: September 1986

REPORTING AGENT: Danger Mouse

WEATHER: Decidedly chilly

DANGER LEVEL: Middling to Murderous

URGENCY: UTTERLY URGENT

COMMENTS FROM COMMANDING OFFICER:

"Terrible nuisance going on over in the old Communist Bloc that we need you chaps to take a look at. The old Russkie leader Mikhail Gorbachev has been acting strangely. Or rather his birthmark has. It's been punching people and attempting to launch intercontinental ballistic missile strikes. Which, as you chaps know, is frowned upon in no uncertain terms by all the other international chappies. Get over there and investigate! How do I turn caps on OH YES THERE WE ARE PLEASE READ THE PRECEDING PARAGRAPH AS THOUGH IT WAS IN CAPS EXCEPT FOR THIS BIT THANK YOU."

AUTHORISING SIGNATURE: *Colonel K.*

DANGER MOUSE:

It was time to grab a phrasebook and zip over to Mother Russia to find out what the stroganoff was going on! Before long we had a tip-off that the Russian leader's birthmark had been recently treated by a doctor with a suspicious name. So we went to investigate this suspicious medical meddler ...

And found this doctor was actually arch-villain Dr Augustus P Crumhorn III!

With the dastardly Crumhorn in custody we uncovered his plot to blow up a new supercomputer made by the American scientists who had built 'DEEP BLUE'.

RUSSIAN PHRASES:

'Oh cripes!'
о, Боже!

'Oh carrot!'
ой морковь!

'Crumbs!'
крошек!

'Rotten egg!'
тухлое яйцо

'Good grief!'
печаль во благо!

Crumhorn had programmed this mathematical machine into being a killing computer. It was to explode during a chess match with Russian grandmaster Garry Kasparov, an event that would lead to an international conflagration. We had to act fast - because the match had begun. After following Kasparov to the lav, we locked him in. Then a quaking Penfold (wearing the Russian's clothes) took Kasparov's place in the match...

We went to ask The Police for assistance.
But they just said they thought
the Russians loved their children too.
Which was no help.

It was dear Penfold who succeeded in
defusing the bomb. Mathematically the
chess computer VERY DEEP BLUE, ALMOST
PURPLE was on a course to total success.
But the choices that Penfold made in
the game (such as bringing all his
pawns back in line an hour into the
game, just to see if he could) had so
little sense to them, that the computer
could not understand them. It could no
longer predict his moves with regards
to the game of chess, and therefore its
programme short-circuited in sheer
confusion.

I was just so hungry all the time, because of all this
talk of prawns. Will I have some prawns then? Or
not? No one seems to want to answer me. Hello?

BRENT COUNCIL
PRESS RELEASE
Statue of Danger Mouse to Be Unveiled in Willesden Green

At long last, now that the Confidential Reports can be released, Danger Mouse can receive the recognition that the world's greatest secret agent so richly deserves. Therefore MI-6 is pleased to announce that from next month a bronze statue commemorating Danger Mouse (and his sidekick Penfold) will be erected in Willesden Green, in front of the empty shopfronts where Bejam and Woolworths used to be. You can see (right) an artist's drawing of the statue of Danger Mouse (and his sidekick Penfold) ahead of the statue's unveiling next month.

Gleam of brilliance

Impressive polish

Defiant expression – impervious to fear

Bad reviews from local populace

Heroic stance

This is probably saying something nice, like 'Penfold's the best!'

Bulletproof skin – just like in real life eh?

Glow of success

Shining beacon of hope

::::::::::INCOMING MESSAGE::::::::::

Don't want to give away any national secrets, do I? So I had to give this the once-over before releasing it, to make sure no details get out that could compromise our security. Nevertheless I'm sure you can see we all eat jolly well here at HQ! Except for the ------- of course.

MI-6 STAFF CANTEEN

MENU

MAIN DISHES

▓▓▓ in the Hole:
Long pink meaty tubes of delicious ▓▓▓ pricked with forks, grilled to bursting then dipped in a moist ▓▓▓ and baked, served with ▓▓▓ sauce.

Shepherd's ▓▓▓
Hot meat mixed with ▓▓▓ and ▓▓▓ then topped with creamy ▓▓▓, placed in a dish and roasted for forty minutes until bubbling. Served with two veg.

Don't know why, but I've suddenly lost my appetite today, DM

DESSERTS

▓▓▓ and ▓▓▓
A moist, pink delicacy made with ▓▓▓ and ▓▓▓ from a ▓▓▓. Suitable for ▓▓▓. Most UNsuitable for ▓▓▓.

I know what you mean. Let's go next door and get a load of hot spicy  Now YOU'RE at it!

CASE #10

MISSION CODE NAME:

WHO FRAMED DANGER MOUSE?

DATE: June 1987	**REPORTING AGENT:** Danger Mouse

LOCATION: Everywhere! Nowhere? Somewhere.

TEXTURE: Sandpaper

DANGER LEVEL: Dangerous as you like. No wait, MORE dangerous than you'd like

URGENCY: MEGA URGENT

COMMENTS FROM COMMANDING OFFICER:

"WELL NOW WHAT'S ALL THIS? CARTOON CHARACTERS ARE BEING KIDNAPPED ALL OVER THE PLACE. INCLUDING YOU, DM! AND ME TOO, DASH IT! IT'S LUCKY I'VE GOT THIS RECORDING DEVICE IN MY LAPEL DISGUISED AS A MEMBERSHIP BADGE FOR THE M.C.C.! WHEN YOU RECEIVE THIS MESSAGE I INSIST THAT YOU BREAK OUT OF INCARCERATION, FIND OUT WHAT THE JOLLY HOCKEY STICKS IS GOING ON AND PUT A SWIFT END TO IT! MESSAGE ENDS! HMM. THERE'S NO STOP BUTTON. I REALLY WISH I HAD MY HANDS FREE TO SCRATCH MY"

AUTHORISING SIGNATURE: *Colonel K.*

DANGER MOUSE:

It all started when I put Penfold
in front of the telly to watch his
favourite cartoons while I prepared
his favourite dinner of chips-on-jam-
on-toast. When he made an awful fuss
I thought he'd knocked over his milk,
but then I saw the television...

All the best cartoon shows were
still on telly, but one after the
other, they came on empty! First
SuperTed, then Bananaman, then
He—Man — all just backgrounds!
DM took one look at it
and realised that the
main characters had
been kidnapped. 'I hope no other
beloved cartoon heroes will be next,'
he said — and at that moment our post-box
headquarters filled with gas and we conked out!

When we came round we were in a
rather rustic-looking dwelling that
Penfold informed me (after about ten
'Cor!'s and twenty 'Well I never!'s
and a few dozen 'Who'd have believed
it!'s) was called Castle Greyskull.
We had been tied up and left in a
dungeon, which was hardly unusual,
but after glancing around the room I
noticed the boulder opposite looking
at me in a funny way. 'Agent 57, if I
am not much mistaken?' I asked. 'He's
lost it at last!' said Penfold. But
then the boulder replied, 'There's no
fooling you, Danger Mouse,' at which
Penfold squeaked, and said, 'Now I'VE
lost it!' and fainted. It was indeed
Agent 57, that master of disguise,
after all. In a trice he had helped
us escape our bonds, and the prison.

We hijacked some camels and made our way across
the cartooniverse, stopping by Thundera to see if the
Thundercats were in — but they were gone too. We
also stopped by Cybertron, but Optimus Prime and the
other Transformers were nowhere to be seen.

At last we came across an abandoned
van, which Penfold assured me was
the Mystery Machine. I told him that
didn't explain anything. But he said
it was the van Scooby Doo and his
friends travelled around in. This was
getting worse than I thought - was any
cartoon character safe?

DM deduced that if the villain was taking over
the cartoon world, he must have based himself in
— its headquarters The Cartoon Hall of Fame.
So that's where we sped at once!

No surprise, that's where the green
devil was, and we saw at once why.
All the kidnapped characters had been
entered into the Hall of Fame, but
not Greenback himself. And so he was
engaged in an attempt to have all their
names scrubbed out, and replaced with
his own. Except as he tried to make the
first alteration, it seemed the fabric
of reality (or cartooneality) would not
accept his changes!

We soon realised this cartooniverse was ruled over by the gods of animation, who suddenly appeared in the sky: Walt Disney, Chuck Jones and Ray Harryhausen, explaining that the empty chair next to them was for Hayao Miyazaki. They would not allow this crime to stand as it went against the laws of cartoons which are, admittedly, stretchy.

And so they plucked Baron Greenback up and consigned him to cartoon hell. Luckily we were in the cartoon universe rather than the scriptwriter's one, where this 'deus ex machina' could never be allowed to occur. Greenback disappeared screaming into the abyss to join Scrappy Doo, Jar Jar Binks, Snarf and many blood-curdling others. Serves him right!

Are you sure we should be released right now, DM? It's just I was having an enchanting chat with Jessica Rabbit ...

::::::INCOMING MESSAGE::::::

WHY, THOSE CHAPS HAVE TO DASH ABOUT THE EARTH LIKE MAD THINGS, SO AS YOU CAN SEE THEIR PASSPORTS GET QUITE A BATTERING. FUNNY HOW DIFFERENT THE STAMPS ON PENFOLD AND DM'S PASSPORTS ARE, COME TO THINK OF IT, SEEING AS THEY ARE ALWAYS TOGETHER ...

COLONEL K

1-00865-976432
Call me, darlink!
Olglinska

Ah, dear Olglinska – I remember we met in the casino at Reykjavik

A splash of champagne →

88

BOARDING
FIRST CLASS

FIRST CLASS

GATE:
7

SEAT

GATE:
20

IG PASS

ARDING PASS
GER TICKET AND BAGGAGE CHECK

FIRST CLASS

BOARDING PASS
FIRST CLASS

GATE	GATE CLOSES	SEAT
7	19:30	25b

Class
First Class

GATE:

WALES
ACCESS
DENIED

WILLESDEN
GREEN
FEE PAID

WILLESDEN
GREEN
FEE PAID

NEASDEN
P.I.A./A.I.P

WILLESDEN
GREEN
FEE PAID

WILLESDEN
GREEN
FEE PAID

WILLESDEN
GREEN
FEE PAID

WILLESDEN
GREEN
FEE PAID

WILLESDEN
GREEN
FEE PAID

WILLESDEN
GREEN
FEE PAID

1-74637-498743
To our most frequent customer,
come back soon!

Love,
The staff at
the Willesden Green
Spud-u-Like

10

11

↑
blob of custard

↖
Lost to myself
again!!!

CASE #11

MISSION CODE NAME:

SOMETHING FISHY'S GOING ON

DATE: October 1987

REPORTING AGENT: Danger Mouse

LOCATION: BRITAIN! Blessed Sceptred Isle and Centre of Industry!

PAGE COUNT: 356 with two picture sections

DANGER LEVEL: DANGEROUSEST of all the DANGER Levels!

URGENCY: UNQUESTIONABLY URGENT!

COMMENTS FROM COMMANDING OFFICER:

"WILD WEATHER AFOOT, DM! THIS RUM WEATHER PRESENTER FELLOW ASSURES US THERE'S TO BE NO STORM AND YET NEXT THING WE KNOW OUR WASHING'S BEEN BLOWN OFF THE LINE AND THERE'S A TREE STICKING THROUGH THE ROOF! AND WE'D ONLY JUST HAD THE TILING RE-DONE! THERE'S A CONSPIRACY! GET OUT THERE AND FIND OUT WHO'S RESPONSIBLE! IT'S GETTING ME UNDER THE WEATHER!"

AUTHORISING SIGNATURE: *Colonel K.*

First DM and I watched the weather report where this suspicious character, named Michael Man-not-Fish, who looked most decidedly like a fish wearing a false moustache to me, told us there was definitely no storm coming. Then we stepped out of the front door to get clattered by gale-force winds! There were cars flying through the air and boats landing on the top of cathedrals!

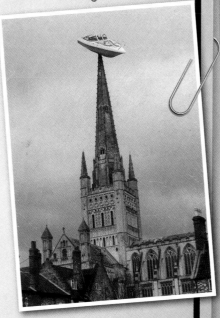

DANGER MOUSE:

> I decided we should expose the plan of this sinister 'weatherfish' by inviting him on my favourite game show, *Blind Date*. To aid us I called in Agent 57 who dressed as Timmy Mallett and then he asked the three of us questions …

TRANSCRIPT OF BLIND DATE EPISODE #65 FROM OCTOBER 1987:

Cilla: Alright our chook, go ahead with your final question.

Michael Man-not-Fish: Do I have to read this?

Cilla: Yes love, of course you do.

Michael Man-not-Fish: (Uncertainly) Well, okay … I'm going to ask Date Number One. If you were a megalomaniac trying to take over the world with a secret plan, what would it be?

Date Number One (a.k.a. Agent 57): Well, Michael, if I was going to take over the world I'd kidnap some nuclear warheads and hold them to ransom. Because the real nuclear holocaust is taking place in my heart … for you. And the fallout will last for a million years!

Cilla: Oooo! He sounds interesting!

Michael Man-not-Fish: Hmm, I dunno, Cilla. Can I ask that question to Date Number Two please?

Date Number Two (a.k.a. Penfold): Michael, I'm so glad you asked. Because if I was to take over the world I'd do it by inventing a computer virus that took over all the computers in the world and make everything come to a dead stop until my demands were met. Because you see, my heart comes to a stop, when I think about you.

Cilla: Ey well e's a bit of alright in't 'e?

Michael Man-not-Fish: Yyyyyes, although from his voice I'm not quite sure he's my type … Can I hear what the answer would be from Date Number Three please?

Date Number Three (Danger Mouse, of course): If I took over the world I would disguise myself as a weatherman and trick the whole world into thinking the weather was going to be clement when in fact there is an enormous storm coming, because I am in secret a Sea Monster who wants to control the whole planet from beneath the waves!

Michael Man-not-Fish: Why, that's exactly like me! A perfect match!

Cilla: It looks like I'm gonna have to buy a hat!

[The partition draws back]

[Agent 57 dressed as Timmy Mallett startles the fishy weatherfish by jumping forward and repeatedly thwumping him on the head with his mallet.]

DM: We've got you, evil Michael Man-not-Fish-But-is-Actually-Fish!

Penfold: We should have really thought of it when we heard that suspicious name!

DM: I thought it was Welsh …

Cilla: Surprise Surprise, chuck, you're going to prison for a long time!

and beautiful and self-possessed; and she was as scornful of me as if she had been one-and-twenty, and a queen.

We went into the house by a side door—the great front entrance had two chains across it outside—and the first thing I noticed was, that the passages were all dark, and that she had left a candle burning there. She took it up, and we went through more passages and up a staircase, and still it was all dark, and only the candle lighted us.

At last we came to the door of a room, and she said, 'Go in.'

I answered, more in shyness than politeness, 'After you, miss.'

To this, she returned: 'Don't be ridiculous, boy; I am not going in.' And scornfully walked away, and—what was worse —took the candle with her.

This was very uncomfortable, and I was half afraid. However, the only thing to be done being to knock at the door, I knocked, and was told from within to enter. I entered, therefore, and found myself in a pretty large room, well lighted with wax candles. No glimpse of daylight was to be seen in it. It was a dressing-room, as I supposed from the furniture, though much of it was of forms and uses then quite unknown to me. But prominent in it was a draped table with a gilded looking-glass, and that I made out at first sight to be a fine lady's dressing-table.

Whether I should have made out this object so soon, if there had been no fine lady sitting at it, I cannot say. In an arm-chair, with an elbow resting on the table and her head leaning on that hand, sat the strangest lady I have ever seen, or shall ever see.

She was dressed in rich materials—satins, and lace, and silks—all of white. Her shoes were white. And she had a long white veil dependent from her hair, and she had bridal flowers in her hair, but her hair was white. Some bright jewels sparkled on her neck and on her hands, and some other jewels lay sparkling on the table. Dresses, less splendid than the dress she wore, and half-packed trunks, were scattered about. She had not quite finished dressing, for she had but one shoe on—the other was on the table near her hand—her veil was but half arranged, her watch and chain were not put on, and some lace for her bosom lay with those trinkets, and with her handkerchief, and gloves, and some flowers, and a Prayer-book, all confusedly heaped about the looking-glass.

It was not in the first few moments that I saw all these things, though I saw more of them in the first moments than might be supposed. But, I saw that everything within my view which ought to be white, had been white long ago, and had lost its lustre, and was faded and yellow. I saw that the bride within the bridal dress had withered like the dress, and like the flowers, and had no brightness left but the brightness of her sunken eyes. I saw that the dress had been put upon the rounded figure of a young woman, and that the figure upon which it now hung loose, had shrunk to skin and bone. Once, I had been taken to see some ghastly waxwork at the Fair, representing I know not what impossible personage lying in state. Once, I had been taken to one of our old marsh churches to see a skeleton in the ashes of a rich dress, that had been dug out of a vault under the church pavement. Now, waxwork and skeleton seemed to have dark eyes that moved and looked at me. I should have cried out, if I could.

'Who is it?' said the lady at the table.

'Pip, ma'am.'

'Pip?'

'Mr. Pumblechook's boy, ma'am. Come—to play.'

'Come nearer; let me look at you. Come close.'

It was when I stood before her, avoiding her eyes, that I took note of the surrounding objects in detail, and saw that her watch had stopped at twenty minutes to nine, and that a clock in the room had stopped at twenty minutes to nine.

'Look at me,' said Miss Havisham. 'You are not afraid of a woman who has never seen the sun since you were born?'

I regret to state that I was not afraid of telling the enormous lie comprehended in the answer 'No.'

'Do you know what I touch here?' she said, laying her hands, one upon the other, on her left side.

'Yes, ma'am.' (It made me think of the young man.)

'What do I touch?'

'Your heart.'

'Broken!'

She uttered the word with an eager look, and with strong emphasis, and with a weird smile that had a kind of boast in it. Afterwards, she kept her hands there for a little while, and slowly took them away as if they were heavy.

'I am tired,' said Miss Havisham. 'I want diversion, and I have done with men and women. Play.'

My parents were going to call me Pip, you know.
But they couldn't spell it. That must really give you the pip. eh?

CASE #12

MISSION CODE NAME:

A FRUIT AND NUTCASE

DATE: October 1987

REPORTING AGENT: Danger Mouse

LOCATION: LONDON! Delightful domicile of decorum and delicacy!

TOP SPEED: 136 km/h

DANGER LEVEL: You can't spell VERY DANGEROUS without DANGEROUS, if you know what I mean? You don't? Well, it's DANGEROUS, is what I'm saying.

URGENCY: UNBEARABLY URGENT!

COMMENTS FROM COMMANDING OFFICER:

"GHASTLY GOINGS-ON IN THE CITY, DM! THE COUNTRY'S ASSETS HAVE BEEN LIQUIDATED! IT SEEMS THE GOLD BULLION IN THE BANK OF ENGLAND HAS MELTED AND IS SLOSHING ABOUT THE PLACE - SOME MISERLY MISCREANT HAD REPLACED THE STUFF WITH GOLD-COVERED CHOCOLATE! THEY'RE CALLING IT SQUIDGY-BROWN MONDAY! GET ON OVER THERE AND FIND OUT WHAT'S AFOOT! I KNOW WHAT A FOOT IS PENFOLD, PUT YOUR SHOES BACK ON AND GET OUT THERE WITH DM!"

AUTHORISING SIGNATURE: *Colonel K.*

DANGER MOUSE:

> First off I had to infiltrate
> the Stock Exchange dressed as a
> stockbroker. It was explained to me
> that owing to the natural laws of
> observational comedy I had to take an
> outlandishly enormous mobile telephone
> with me, which I did - it was so large
> I had to carry it in a suitcase.

DM seemed very worried about what was going on, but I had been on a trip to the cinema the previous night and so I knew that 'greed is good'. Therefore I was refusing to share any of my strawberry bonbons with him. However when Colonel K asked me to telephone DM, I couldn't make hide nor hair of what he was talking about with this 'mobile home' business. 'No!' he ended up shouting, 'it's a mobile telephone, a cell phone! Cell! Cell! Cell!'

Unfortunately this set off quite the
panic in the city and precipitated a
stock market crash that came to be known
as 'Even Squidgier-Brown Tuesday'.
Hundreds and hundreds of pounds were
wiped off the exchange at once. But in
the panic I overheard people talking
and discovered what was afoot. With
the change of the country's wealth from
gold to chocolate everyone was being
encouraged to invest in sweets …

Soon we knew that the
evil toad (and I mean that
literally, he is one) Baron
Greenback had changed his
name to Dr Sweet-Tooth, the
evil dentist, who dwelled in a
secretive castle. Not only had
he stolen the real gold but
he'd flooded the market
with chocco to make a
further mint from fixing
everyone's teeth!

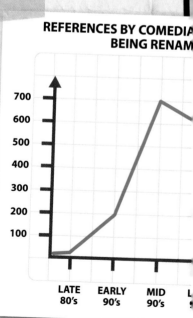

REFERENCES BY COMEDIA
BEING RENAM

700		
600		
500		
400		
300		
200		
100		
LATE 80's	EARLY 90's	MID 90's

As we approached the castle of the evil dentist, we discovered it was well protected. We sheltered behind rocks while we were bombarded with sherbert-fountain grenades and flying saucers with lethally sharpened edges. Next we crept through the swamp at the front of the castle, which was infested with booby-traps made from candy necklaces, and tried to avoid getting caught in webs made from Curly Wurlys. We all stopped short of the treacherous logs across the stream that looked like Cadbury Flakes.

But once we'd made our way through the swamp rather than storm the front of the castle, clever old DM had the idea of donning a cloth cap and going round the back, claiming to have a new delivery of Caramacs and Refreshers. Greenback let us in at once and when he saw we'd rumbled his plan, he tried to flee out of a window — in the process falling into his own moat — a fate worse than death as it was filled with Angel Delight!

Look In EXCLUSIVE
DANGER MOUSE INTERVIEW!

Since we've been in the public eye, many have wanted to know the secrets of our daily existence. The make of my roll-neck white sweaters and trousers, for instance. (They are, in fact, hand-sewn for me by my special chap on Savile Row. Dashed clever he is too.) Many have also been asking Penfold for the name of his ophthalmologist, so they can steer clear of him. Good idea too.

One thing we are more than happy to share, however, is our favourite recipes. First, here's mine:

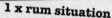

Danger Mouse's Favourite Recipe

- 1 x rum situation
- A handful of clues
- 2 x dashing heroes (second hero optional, doesn't have to be as good as the first)
- 1 x medium-sized mystery
- 1 x clue, almost invisible to the naked eye
- 1 x large, spotted, green amphibian villain with optional sidekicks

First take the rum situation, leave it to simmer for a while over a low heat and mix in the medium-sized mystery. Add the dashing heroes (or hero – one will suffice in truth) then sprinkle over a handful of clues.

Add the amphibian villain, mix well and place into a hot oven and a thrilling finale will result in a matter of minutes.

Voila! So you have my Recipe for Excitement and Adventure!

Penfold's Favourite Recipe

- 1 x egg
- 2 x rashers of bacon
- 3 x slices of toast
- 1 x tin of beans
- 1 x pot of chocolate spread
- 1 x pot of lemon curd
- 1 x baked potato
- 3 x slices black pudding

First, fry the egg and bacon, and put them in the oven to keep warm.

Second, heat the beans on the hob with a dash of ground pepper and Worcestershire sauce.

Third, put the toast on and open the lids of the chocolate spread and lemon curd in readiness.

Next, answer an urgent telephone call from your Uncle Murgatroyd. Talk to him for several minutes, assuring him that the world has not ended, and that it is simply that his television is on the blink. Make a rash promise to go and visit him in Rutland in the next few months. Feel guilty that you won't follow up on this.

Now go back to the cooker to discover that the baked beans have turned black and fused themselves to the saucepan, and the egg and bacon were at too high a heat and have burned. Remove them and fan desperately at the smoke alarm as it goes off for ten minutes.

Now starving and exhausted, heat up a leftover baked potato from the fridge and fry some slices of black pudding. Retrieve the cold toast from the toaster and then spread the lemon curd and chocolate spread over the baked potato and black pudding, and pour brown sauce over the cold toast, because you're not thinking straight.

Eat the resulting mess anyway because you're so hungry, then retire to your bed with a funny tummy for the rest of the day. This is a meal I call BREAKFAST.

CASE #13

MISSION CODE NAME:

TOMORROW'S WHIRLED

DATE: May 1988

REPORTING AGENT: Danger Mouse

LOCATION: LONDON! Engine of empire, fulcrum of finance!

TEMPERATURE: 170° C for twenty minutes, pierce film lid

DANGER LEVEL: Oh I don't know, maybe VERY DANGEROUS INDEED

URGENCY: EXTRA URGENT

COMMENTS FROM COMMANDING OFFICER:

"TERRIBLY CONFUSING OCCURRENCE: DM, PENFOLD AND I FIND OURSELVES CLAPPING EACH OTHER ON THE BACK SAYING JOB-WELL-DONE, ONLY WE CAN'T REMEMBER WHAT THE JOLLY OLD CASE IS THAT WE JUST SOLVED! SOMEONE'S BEEN STEALING TIME. AND INTO THE BARGAIN - THE CROWN JEWELS HAVE GONE MISSING! THERE IS ONLY ONE AGENT FOR THE CASE! SORRY PENFOLD - I MEANT TWO, OF COURSE. TWO. DON'T LOOK AT ME LIKE THAT."

AUTHORISING SIGNATURE: *Colonel K.*

DANGER MOUSE:

First we popped over to the
laboratory of Dr Squawkencluck,
to see what he had to say. I told
him that someone was messing with
our clocks and he introduced me
to a brand new invention of his,
straight off the assembly line:
the DE-TIME-INATOR machine. Using
this, he said, we could shoot back
in time and find out what was
going on!

When we arrived in the past I was transfixed!
Not that I'd been transbroken in the first place.
'Oh DM!' I cried. 'Isn't it fascinating to have a glimpse
into the way things once were! How privileged we are!
Can we possibly hope to riddle the mysteries
of deepest, darkest ancient past?
Hark! Doth I spotteth a mighty dinosaur?'

I told Penfold to stop being so
silly, it wasn't a dinosaur,
just someone walking their
Labrador. After all, we'd only
travelled back to the previous
Thursday. I sat him down with a
cheese sandwich while I did some
investigating ('sandwiches from
the past taste so DIFFERENT, DM!'
'Well we've gone back in time
so I expect for once the cheese
is within its use-by date')
but before I'd had a chance to
begin, Penfold was pointing at
the television and gesticulating,
garbling incoherently through his
mouthful of cheese sandwich.

What did I see but the villainous toad himself, Baron
   Greenback, on *Tomorrow's World*! It seemed they had
invited him on to demonstrate an exciting new device.
It was a huge futuristic-looking gun, and when he pulled
      the trigger it made everyone's minds go blank!

Lucky Dr Squawkencluck had given us protective ear muffs for just this contingency (not that Penfold necessarily needed them, his mind being rather blank already). Needless to say, we zipped across town to the Tower of London, and caught the dreadful Baron in the act of nabbing the old crown and sceptre.

While I distracted the fiendish frog with some entirely intentional falling over and getting caught up in a giant suit of armour, DM switched the settings on his gun so that when Greenback turned his weapon on us and fired, saying, 'Say hello to my little friend, White Wonder!' he was flung far into the future!

The Queen was frightfully grateful, but when Penfold suggested we both get knighted for our services, she said we could get knotted!

In the future, we will all carry devices with which we can order food, go shopping, meet romantic partners, make films, listen to millions of different music tracks and look at street maps from anywhere on earth!

Oh dear, Penfold, you've really lost it this time.

COLONEL K

::::::::INCOMING MESSAGE::::::::

Jolly Good Show rescuing the Crown Jewels like that, boys! Where would the country be without 'em? My brother in law had an operation on the Crown Jewels, you know. Didn't have to go to the palace though — just his local hospital. Very mysterious.

H.R. QUES
Are you fit to

Answer the below and then hand in your form to your commanding officer. Officers scoring lower than 3 points will be placed on stapler-watching duty unless Penfold scores that again, in which case he will continue stapler-watching duty.

1. DANGER

While you are in the bank depositing a cheque (or drawing out some money to buy a nice primrose for your mother because Mothering Sunday is approaching – although this is by the by) a masked madman breaks in brandishing a gun and demanding cash. DO YOU:

☐ a) Distract him by reflecting the sun's rays off a pair of dark glasses, disable him, and save the day, with much shouting and merriment?

☐ b) Hide your head in a bag and call for your mummy, begging that your last meal won't be the stinky cheese and egg sandwich you had for lunch?

☐ c) Start singing the overture from Oklahoma! while doing backflips?

2. SPYCRAFT

You are in a foreign country on assignment. When you return to your hotel room you notice that some things in your room have been moved. DO YOU:

- [ ] a) Dust the place down for fingerprints with the kit you have hidden in the heel of your shoe, and then run the prints through the computer you have concealed in your dashingly handsome eye-patch. Then, armed with the identities of the miscreants, hunt them down and put them behind bars, to much cheering and congratulations?

- [ ] b) Sit down on the bed, scratch your nose, watch a bit of television and then order a schnitzel on room service. When it arrives you eat it with ketchup and start writing some postcards?

- [ ] c) Run screaming from the room until you reach the bar, where you drink large amounts of vodka before telling a chair that you love it, eventually getting locked out of the hotel and sleeping at a bus stop?

2

3. INTELLIGENCE

You have received a report that a dangerous fugitive has moved into the area and is thought to be trying to buy a bomb. DO YOU:

a) Disguise yourself as an arms dealer (which works seamlessly, as your disguises always do, you clever handsome devil you) and sell a device to the fugitive which is actually full of custard. Meaning he gets caught and makes a mess of his nice suit in the bargain (cue cheers, awards, adoration from the public)?

b) Ask Danger Mouse what to do, and then while he does it, sit in the car and do the Word Search in The Dandy?

c) Change your name to Bertie McBertie Oh The What What Soup on My Tie Carrot-Cake McGherkin Trousers, and dress as a flamingo, ostentatiously sipping tea in the food hall at Harrods?

DM — telephone message from Prime Minster of Japan. He sez they're being held hostage under threat of ~~unclear~~ nuclear catastrophe, they need you're help very urgent — next twenty minutes. Leaving you this note in case you come home as I have gone out walking the tortoise and to buy milk.

Penfold x

4. EQUIPMENT

You have been given a special piece of equipment that looks rather like a laser but the instruction manual has gone missing. DO YOU:

a) Scan it with the Super Spy Mini Scanner you bought from Argos. Seeing it's an all-powerful laser, you decide to try it out on the alien space craft trying to attack Buckingham Palace. It works a treat, and the Queen gives you a little peck on the head in thanks, crowds cheering etc?

b) Say, 'I wonder what that does' and press the button next to which is printed 'CAUTION'. When it blows an enormous hole in the wall, scream 'by 'eck!' and hide under the bed?

c) Take it for a walk in Hyde Park, on a leash. Show it the ducks and the trees, and introduce it to the other pets. Forget it on the bus, and then not worry about it afterwards, assuming someone will find a use for it. Then watch CEEFAX for eleven hours because you find it gripping and want to know what happens next?

ANSWERS:

If you answered mostly a) you are Danger Mouse
If you answered mostly b) you are Penfold
If you answered mostly c) I don't know who you are, but you are a decidedly odd fish and I'm not sure that spying is really for you. Perhaps consider the theatre.

CASE #14

MISSION CODE NAME:

REVENGE IS SWEETS

DATE: November 1989

REPORTING AGENT: Danger Mouse

LOCATION: BERLIN! ROME! PARIS! All the cultural capitals of the world!

STAKES: High

STEAKS: Medium Rare

DANGER LEVEL: As dangerous as a spillage of liquid danger in a danger factory

URGENCY: UTTERLY URGENT

COMMENTS FROM COMMANDING OFFICER:

"A DAY FOR HAPPINESS AND GLAD TIDINGS! THE FALL OF THE BERLIN WALL! EXCEPT IT'S NOT QUITE WHAT YOU THINK. THE BERLIN WALL HASN'T BEEN DISMANTLED, IT'S FALLEN DOWN BECAUSE SOME JOHNNY WITH A FUNNY IDEA HAS TURNED IT INTO BATTENBERG CAKE! THE EIFFEL TOWER'S BEEN TRANSFORMED INTO ECLAIRS! AND THE LEANING TOWER OF PISA HAS FALLEN OVER AND ITS TOPPINGS HAVE GONE EVERYWHERE! IT'S UP TO YOU TO SORT THIS OUT! AND FOR HEAVEN'S SAKE BRING ME BACK A SLICE!"

AUTHORISING SIGNATURE: *Colonel K.*

Just as Colonel K finished his broadcast, we caught the villain at his tricks — the Sistine Chapel was dripping from the ceiling after being turned into gelato! We traced the energy beam and located the unscrupulous amphibian Baron Greenback in an artist's garret in London. Soon we discovered that he had been taken with artistic ambition, and wanted to transform landmarks that had been depicted by other artists so he could make them his own, and become a famous artist. Naturally he wore a beret.

DANGER MOUSE:

Suddenly I had a thought: what's
the most frequently reproduced
painting in the whole of Britain?
(Penfold suggested it was
the 'remarkably lifelike and
sensitively rendered' portrait he
had in his downstairs lavatory of
dogs playing poker by van Gogh.
Why do I ever ask him?) It was the
Queen's face, of course! On every
stamp in the land! And hadn't I
just read that she was about to
sit for a new official portrait,
to be painted by an unknown
artist? (I had. Don't know why I
put that in question form.)

We roared across London to Buck Pal and got there just
in time. When Greenback arrived, he crept towards Her
Majesty with feral or, rather, toadal stealth. Despite
the danger, of course Her Majestic Queenness sat with
perfectly straightened spine and fearless demeanour
as he approached...

As the arch-toad leapt out to secure her for her portrait with the words, 'Fear not, my lady, I shall give you a true transformation …' he was shocked to find his head sticking through a canvas. You see, he had not been approaching the real monarch at all, but a portrait! One so perfectly painted as to be indistinguishable from the real person, and practically a photograph. It had of course been painted in ten minutes flat … by yours truly!

Yes, he didn't half harp on about his painting. 'Didn't I do that painting quickly?' he asked afterwards. 'Yes, DM,' I said. 'And isn't it amazing that the painting was so good, Greenback really thought it was her?' 'Yes, DM,' I said, 'You are clever.' He didn't stop all night and next day.

Anyway, while Greenback was all confused with the portrait round his head, the real Queen (who had been posing in a hole in the wall behind where a portrait usually hung) fired a sleep dart at him to make him dizzy, then set her corgis on him. To Greenback - a toad - these were enormous slavering beasts, and so he ran screaming into the distance, begging for mercy.

For weeks, Danger Mouse kept on about how perfect the portrait he had painted was, and how amazing that he had managed to fool Greenback with it, and how that meant that it was clearly so much better than the portrait Greenback would have come up with — eventually I drowned it out by putting my head under a pillow.

PENFOLD'S 'LIST OF REASONS WHY I AM BETTER THAN DM'

- I finish my dinner before him. Sometimes before he's started.
- I always let him have the bath first because I do not use it except on 6 April every year.
- I came in the top three in the Willesden Green hamster nose-picking contest five years running 1986–90. He was not even in the top twenty!
- I don't even need to have a driving licence because I have my own chauffeur name DM.
- He is a judo red belt. But I am a karate black belt! As long as I don't wash it, when it becomes a He-Man and the Masters of the Universe belt again.
- Girls don't respect him like they do me. Wherever we go they throw their stockings, knickers and garterbelts at him! How embarrassing! Me they respect enough to leave alone.

SECRET SERVICE **OFFICIAL COLOUR SWATCHES**

The Secret Service takes care of all your household needs. Therefore in 1984 they released a chart of officially approved paint colours

CODED MESSAGE

SILENCER

SUNBURN

POISON

ZEBRA

CERTAIN DEATH

SUBTERFUGE

CAMOUFLAGE

DARING ESCAPE

HIDDEN LAIR

They could be ordered through central services!

ACTION

PENFOLD'S BEDROOM

We only had the walls painted white six months ago!

118

SECRET SERVICE

H.R. QUESTIONNAIRE:
Psychic Competition

Many spy networks around the world use psychics to get crucial information. Now you can test yourself to see if you would qualify as a psychic!

First, look at this blank page and see if you can psychically detect what picture we intended to put on it:

ANSWER: THE TAJ MAHAL

As the Television Series came to an end in the early 1990s, I was free to explore Hollywood and a multitude of exciting opportunities. Penfold was due to join me, but owing to misreading the address on the postcard I sent him, ended up moving to Holyhead in North Wales, where he lived for the rest of the 1990s, working on the ferry. I, however, appeared in many motion pictures that proved to be veritable hits on the VHS market.

HONEY, I DEFECTED THE KIDS (1991): After a dreadful mix-up over the labelling of a large package he is supposed to be sending to Soviet Ukraine while simultaneously helping his children in a game of hide-and-go-seek, fond father Rick Moranis accidentally posts his children to the USSR! In desperation, he calls on a cool, suave mouse spy to save the day and repatriate his offspring before his wife returns from a weekend away at a spa. I need not add, I trust, that some comical hijinks ensue.

LAWNMOWER MOUSE (1993): In which I played an academically challenged mouse who was sent into a virtual reality to save the world, gaining the skills of a super-genius in so doing, and solving the world cheese shortage.

USTERS *Video*

FALLING DOWN MOUSE (1994): In which I played a buttoned-up middle class mouse with an office job who, on his drive home one day, loses patience with modern life. He gets home and writes several strongly worded letters to the Daily Telegraph, which vents his anger splendidly, then he drinks his cocoa and goes to bed in a good mood.

SHOWMICE 2: LEAVING MOUSE VEGAS (1996): In which I played a disreputable impresario running a nightly show at a discerning gentlemen's members' club. Protective of the lady mice who are appearing on my show, I end up coming face to face with a nefarious mobster fat cat and enter into a game of cat-and-mouse. Or should that be … mouse-and-cat? (Yes, it should.)

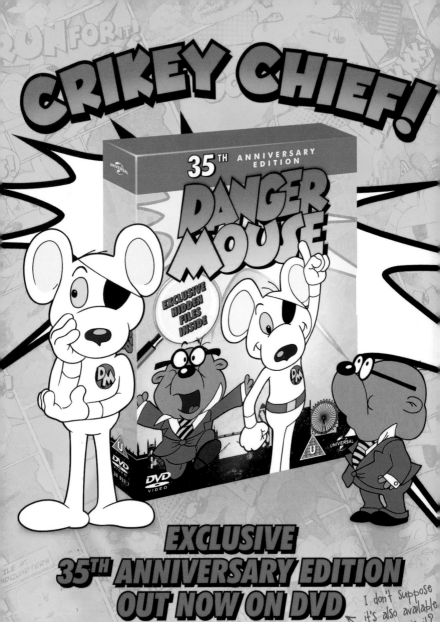

I don't suppose it's also available on VHS, is it?

• BECOME A POSTAL RESIDENT AT THE •

DANGER MOUSE RETIREMENT VILLAGE!

Are you a super-fan of the White Wonder in his original incarnation? Have you been desperate to find out what he was up to all this time he was away? Then you can JOIN the exciting new club!

For a modest monthly subscription fee, you can:

❖ Receive monthly newsletters about what DM is up to, including many rambling anecdotes about the good old days!

❖ Keep tabs on his latest golf scores!

❖ Read humorous reports on him catching up with other old spy friends, and hear them moaning about the boredom of retirement!

❖ Mark his declining health with our patented DM™ doll, with a deteriorating hip joint, expanding belly and detachable teeth!

❖ Send postcards on his behalf to grandchildren whose names and birthdays he can't quite get right!

❖ As an elite member of the Danger Mouse Retirement Village you get the right to pen one letter each month moaning about something in your own life and see if it gets on the Retirement Village Monthly Meeting Agenda. Topics might include: the impoliteness of young people these days, infuriating modern electronic devices, and cold calls offering you accident insurance payouts.

SEND your self-addressed envelope and a cheque for £6.88 to Greenback Enterprises, PO Box 8977, Alberta, Canada.

Applicants must be over 120 years old.

QUINN-FLOSSY

AMO AVOCADOUS

ABOUT THE AUTHOR

Sir Arthur Stuyvesant Quinn-Flossy IV (Bart.) won the bronze award in the 1941 under-fourteens championship for salmon fishing (freestyle) in Clackmannanshire. One of the twentieth century's most prolific poets, he was voted Britain's Most Hated Aristocrat in 1978 because he appeared on Blankety Blank two days after his wife had been executed by Libyan kidnappers. He has written over four hundred volumes of poetry, and boasts of being able to pen 'up to a dozen ditties between teatime and dinner'. Nevertheless, he has taken a firm stance against the literary establishment, accusing them of 'gross snobbishness' in a 1996 interview on BBC Radio Cumberland. 'They don't understand me, and therefore they fear me', he claimed. He cites his influences as Alexander Pope, Jerry Lee Lewis and Purple Ronnie, and says his finest poem is 'A Limerick About Mr Biscuit the Cat Getting Bored and Doing a Poo on the Piano'.

BIBLIOGRAPHY

A History of Rodents in Espionage, Sir David Mouse, Hampton Bunk, 1934

The Successful Tactical Use of Raspberry Mousse in North African Campaign of World War II, General Montgomery, Cambridge Military Books, 1947

How We Rather Easily Repelled the Use of Raspberry Mousse in the North African Campaign of World War II, Field Marshall Rommel, Fischer Verlag, 1948

Er, I don't Think So? I Think it Worked Quite Well Actually?, General Montgomery, Cambridge, 1949

You Keep Telling Yourself That Mate, Field Marshall Rommel, Fischer, 1950

I think We Both Know Who Won the War, General Montgomery, Cambridge, 1951

That Shut Him Up, General Montgomery, Cambridge, 1952

Making Paté out of the Bishop of Lincoln, Camilla Ostenprot, Macmillan, 1982

Headaches Make Me Find it Hard to Concentrate When Trying to Write This Danger Mouse Book, Bruno Vincent, Virgin, 2016

The Art of War – Inflatable Edition for Bathtime, Sun Tzu, Red Pepper Books, 2011

Villainous Lizards – a Rough Guide for Heroes, Rough Guide Books, 2003

From Eye-patch to Roll-neck: Contemporary Fashion Hints for the Style-Conscious Mouse, Gerald Spinton, Random Mouse Books, 1979

What Makes Me a Jolly Good Spy and No Mistake, Roger Moore, Michael O'Mara, 1981

I am Not a Number: Pro Hints from a Eye-Patch-Wearing Spy Legend, Patrick McGoohan, Prospero Books, 1975

A Merrie Historie of the Uncelebrayted Mouse Who Captured Guy Fawkes, Daniel Defoe, pamphlet, 1609

INDEX